"Those who cannot change their mi
George Bern

THE LEADER'S
ULTIMATE GUIDE
TO SUCCESSFUL
TRANSFORMATION

HOW TO BECOME A
TRANSFORMATIONAL LEADER BY UNLOCKING THE SECRET POWER OF **AQ**
ADAPTABILITY INTELLIGENCE

FEATURING INSIGHTS FROM THE MOST INFLUENCIAL LEADERS IN THE WORLD:
TONY MARTIGNETTI | CAMERON HEROLD | CHARLENE LI | DR. DIANE HAMILTON | GREG VERDINO
TRACY BROWER | BARRY O'REILLY | DR. BENJAMIN HARDY | TOM CHEESEWRIGHT | JOHN D. ANDERSON

ROSS THORNLEY

First published 2022
Adaptai Ltd.

Typeset: CrunchX
Printed and bound by KDP
Cover and illustrations by Ross Thornley

ISBN: 9798360587828

www.AQai.io

ACKNOWLEDGEMENTS

To _AQai_ Mike Raven, and Joe Sale

THE LEADER'S ULTIMATE GUIDE TO SUCCESSFUL TRANSFORMATION

"As leaders we have the responsibility to envision and create a future where we would rejoice in the playground we have built for our children"

Ross Thornley

Author of Moonshot Innovation, Decoding AQ, and The Coach's ultimate guide to leveraging adaptability.

"ACT ALWAYS AS IF THE FUTURE OF THE UNIVERSE DEPENDED ON WHAT YOU DID, WHILE LAUGHING AT YOURSELF FOR THINKING THAT WHATEVER YOU DO MAKES ANY DIFFERENCE."

BUDDHA

CONTENTS

"If you want to know what a man's like, take a good look at how he treats his inferiors, not his equals."

J.K. Rowling

STATE OF PLAY

In times of crisis, we look to leadership. And it's pretty much undeniable that our world is undergoing massive transformation and in many industries, regions, and societies it is in a state of crisis. I don't say this to sound like a doom-touting prophet. The world has been in crisis many times before, and is likely to be in a state of crisis again at some point in the future. In fact, it is in times of crisis that humanity rises. We give birth to the greatest leaders amidst the greatest challenges.

But the crisis of the modern world, the crisis we're facing right now, is unique in the history of the planet. Never before have we been so connected, and so empowered with technology and information—all of which *should* help us deal with the problems our societies face.

But our access to technology and information is part of the problem, isn't it? We've grown so rapidly, accelerated our progress in so many fields in such a short space of time, that the playbook of yesterday is no longer fit for purpose.

According to a 2020 World Economic Forum report[1] and 2021 research by McKinsey and Company[2], owing to the pan-

---

1 https://www.weforum.org/press/2020/10/recession-and-automation-changes-our-future-of-work-but-there-are-jobs-coming-report-says-52c5162fce/

2 https://www.mckinsey.com/business-functions/organization/our-insights/

demic's acceleration of automation:

→ **BY 2025, 85 MILLION JOBS WILL BE LOST.**

→ **BY 2025, 97 MILLION NEW JOBS WILL BE GENERATED.**

→ **40% OF TODAY'S EMPLOYMENT WILL NO LONGER EXIST IN TEN YEARS.**

→ **375 MILLION INDIVIDUALS MAY NEED TO CHANGE JOBS AND OBTAIN NEW SKILLS.**

We're seeing more change in ten years than we saw in the last one-hundred, and we're swiftly approaching the "singularity". As I wrote in *Moonshot Innovation*: "As we approach the technological singularity, the moment in time when artificial superintelligence will abruptly trigger a runaway of technological growth, catalysting unfathomable changes to human civilization, changes we cannot see beyond, **it will in some ways be out of our hands.**" [3]

Now there's a thought that some may find scary.

This pace of change has further widened the adaptability gap—the speed at which we are able to radically re-invent, let-

---

building-workforce-skills-at-scale-to-thrive-during-and-after-
the-covid-19-crisis?cid=repeat-soc-lkn-mip-mck-oth-2109--
&sid=5526889337&linkId=132403241

3 Thornley, Ross; *Moonshot Innovation*; 2019.

go, and re-imagine the processes, behaviours, and skills we require to thrive in this new world.

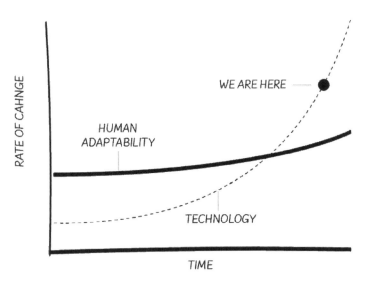

SOURCE: INSPIRED FROM SINGULARITY UNIVERSITY

And what impact is this having on people?

We are asking ourselves more questions, reflecting on what has been, and what we dare to envision for tomorrow. A widespread disconnect; a disconnection from self, a disconnection from the roles and tasks we are doing, a disconnect from misaligned organisational purpose. The global shifts in working relationships is transforming the very fabric of employment.

In 2021 in the UK alone, a record 634,649 people completed the NHS Talking Therapy programme. This is an increase of around 5% on 606,192 in the year before. "Between 1990 and 2013, the number of people suffering from depression and/or anxiety increased by nearly 50%, from 416 million to 615 million."[4] Across the world, shocking numbers of people are struggling with their mental health, and when we look at these numbers we have to bear in mind that there is still a stigma, particularly with men, in reporting on mental health or accessing therapy, so the actual numbers of people struggling with mental health is likely to be much, much higher.

I could quote further sources about the technological trends that are set to destabilise, and transform, our current business models—saying nothing of the ongoing war in the Ukraine and the drastic effect that has had on the cost of living—but I think the mental health statistics give us a shot in the arm of the reality we are swimming in.

We have so much—I truly believe this is an abundant world—yet we seem to be struggling to reap the benefits, or to put it more simply: to get the most out of life.

Joseph Campbell once wrote: "The psychotic drowns in the same waters in which the mystic swims with delight." This might seem a little bit esoteric (and it is) but what this quote highlights is the difference isn't in the *water*, it's in the *person* who's swimming, and their perception and manifestation of their emotions and behaviours.

---

4   Green, David; *The Age of Wellbeing*, 2020.

As leaders, it is our responsibility to help people to swim, rather than drown.

Over the years, there has been significant research and discussion about what a leader is. Leadership is currently one of *the* most popular topics in the fields of business and self-help in publishing. We are inundated with literature exploring leadership: what it is, how we can develop it, how it needs to change, and so on and so forth.

Most writers talking about leadership resort to historical analogs, particularly military leaders, to make their case. Whilst these can be useful on a symbolic and inspirational level, it can often be difficult to apply the actions or thinking of a heroic military commander, or a hyper-successful entrepreneur outlier, to a modern context, especially given how much our world has changed. Most of us, thankfully, are not dealing with military conflict in our day-to-day lives or businesses (though sadly, many people in the East are currently being affected by ongoing warfare). Therefore, to apply military strategy to a modern business problem is unlikely to yield fruitful results. We are seeing a rise in a more human, more inclusive, and heart-centred approach to leadership. Environment is context, and context is everything. We'll return to this theme a number of times throughout this book.

The science of leadership has revealed there are four main theories of leadership emergent: trait, behavioural, contingency, and attributional.

Trait leadership attempts to identify the fixed characteristics of leaders. The idea is that all good leaders would share the same traits or characteristics. Unfortunately, in practice, this is very difficult to establish, and what is considered a good trait in one era of human history is considered a poor one in another. For example, Winston Churchill was once considered the man of the hour who delivered Britain and Europe from the hands of the Nazis in the mid-20th Century. Now, many people are revising their opinions of him in light of his actions in India.

Behavioural theories operate on the principle that an agreed set of traits cannot be established, and therefore focus on *actions*. What do leaders do and can we learn how to do what they do? This theory, too, has now been largely discredited. Ironically, it fell into the same trap as trait-theories: no common set of behaviours or actions could be agreed upon!

Contingency theory marks a change in direction. Recognising the importance of context, contingency theory looks at "situational variables" and how they influence outcomes. For example: why a good decision in one context is an extremely poor one in others. This almost begins to approach the concept of adaptability, because contingency theory is essentially trying to establish that leadership is about matching style, behaviours, and actions to the situation encountered. Whilst contingency theory has produced many insights, the model is so complex that it becomes difficult to apply learnings in any kind of practical context. In other words, it is just that: a brilliant theory, but without any kind of applicable use, yet. However, certainly there is more to explore here, and perhaps AQ provides the necessary missing piece of "action"—but I'm getting ahead of myself.

The last of these, attribution theory, takes another radical sidestep and approaches leadership from a purely perceptual standpoint. In other words, leaders are what we perceive them to be! This theory bizarrely circles us back to trait theory, in one sense, only it is examining traits from the other side, of *those being led* and their perceptions rather than from some kind of empirical measure.

We have also seen a discussion, emergent in the few last decades, of transactional versus transformational leadership. Though these concepts will likely be familiar to you, I will briefly sketch them out here for the purpose of thoroughness:

→ **TRANSACTIONAL LEADERSHIP** tends to be concerned with *management*. It is about setting deadlines, using resources, focusing on process, establishing procedures, and is generally focused on *efficiency*.

→ **TRANSFORMATIONAL LEADERSHIP** tends to be concerned with people and vision. It is about creating a better future, about organisational values, inspiring teams, innovating, and is focused on *effectiveness*.

Naturally, many believe that transformational leadership is the way forward in our time of continual change. But still the question remains: **how** do we become a transformational leader?

Needless to say, the rise in mental health issues, the rapidly accelerating change our societies are going through, and the turmoil of the economy pose significant challenges for any leader. I mean this on two levels. Firstly, our businesses are going to face challenges like never before; we may even be facing challenges we don't fully understand due to the increasing complexity of how technology is transforming industries overnight. And secondly, let us not forget that businesses are organisms composed of people, sometimes hundreds or even thousands of people, and we are going to have to shepherd them through the most significant period of change in human history. And if we don't, we're *all* in deep trouble.

The impact these changes are having on people is evident in the stats I quoted at the very start of this book. But where crisis looms, there is always opportunity. The world needs great leaders to rise up, to help navigate the choppy waters ahead. But leaders too have greater challenges and obstacles to overcome. Something needs to change. Leaders need help, they need to re-imagine their approaches, acquire new tools, and surf the rapid growth of our era, shifting from a confidence found in experience, knowledge, and "having the answers", to confidence through experiments, vulnerability, and learning-out-loud.

AND THIS IS WHERE THE SUPER POWER OF ADAPTABILITY COMES IN.

THE POWER OF ADAPTABILITY

To cope with rapid change, we must develop our ability to not only cope with change but *thrive* with and through constant change. This is what developing our adaptability muscles can unlock. And the great news is all of us are adaptable inherently, it's just that some have built up their skills and curated their environment to harness this resource more than others.

In addition, we each adapt in our own unique way, and understanding our adaption style is critical to manifesting our best selves and unlocking our greatest potential; likewise, understanding the adaption style of our people and teams can give us access to new realms of insight and opportunity.

During periods of transformation and systematic upheaval, the prospect of making changes can feel like a never ending, daunting story. Change can trigger fear, especially for those in leadership positions or positions of significant responsibility, and often, when under stress, humans default to familiar patterns (or whatever solutions worked for us in the past). This is one of many "adaptability paradoxes": when we most need to learn and change, we stick with what we know, often to our detriment.

But why adaptability and not some other concept? In today's interconnected age, we are constantly bombarded from every front with new ideas, information, offerings, and invitations to new communities.

In light of this, it would be easy to see adaptability as a bit of a buzzword. After all, it's taking the world by storm, and with good reason. Just about every major study—from the World Economic Forum, to Deloitte, to Mckinsey, Linkedin and PWC—are placing 'adaptability' as the #1 essential skill of our time.[5]

BUT IN REALITY, ADAPTABILITY IS AN ANCIENT CONCEPT, ONE THAT'S BEEN WITH HUMANITY SINCE THE BEGINNING.

---

5 https://www.linkedin.com/pulse/why-best-coaches-world-learning-how-leverage-adaptability-businesses-/

Baron de Montesquieu observed, commenting on the unique success of the Roman Empire, "[The Romans] always gave up their own practices as soon as they found better ones."

Most empires are destroyed because of their inherant inflexlibility and xenophobia; they see any culture other than their own as a threat that must be subjugated. This close-mindedness cuts one off from learning opportunities. But the Romans were different. They stole, adopted, and integrated from different cultures repeatedly. So long as it improved upon something, they were happy to get rid of the old and embrace the new. We can see this in virtually every aspect of their culture, even their religion!

Cultures (and indeed businesses) that refuse to let go of the old tend to die off. Even the mighty Spartans, who at one time were the greatest fighting force in the ancient world, were destroyed because they failed to adapt to new technological innovation. The Battle of Leuctra in 371 BC saw the defeat of Sparta at the hands of Thebes, and among the many strategies deployed by the Theban general, Epaminondas, were slingshots and light-cavalry. These technological developments threw the Spartans, who had been entrenched in a very specific method of warfare for seven hundred years. Arguably the Spartans were in decline long before that battle, with a diminishing population and increasingly strained ties with other Greek city-states, all due to their inflexible mindset. Their relationship with tradition was extraordinarily rigid—understandably given how much success it brought them in the beginning—but ultimately this rigidity spelled their doom.

So, adaptability is the key to swimming in the waters of life and change.

WHY AQ IS A CHEAT-CODE FOR LEADERSHIP

At AQai, we use a tripartite model of Adaptability in order to measure AQ (or "Adaptability Quotient"). We call this the A.C.E. model: Ability, Character, and Environment.

We'll cover Ability and Character in time, but for now we'll start with the third: **Environment**. It might seem strange to start here, but the reality is that much of our suffering or success comes from disharmony or harmony with our environment.

Our environment is a context in which we behave and act. If our behaviour is incongruous with or inconsiderate of the context, then we are likely to run into problems. This is precisely the issue the modern world is facing. We're still behaving as if we're in environment X, but the world has moved on, we're now in environment Y. Technology and our environment are ahead of us, and the gap is going to keep widening unless we radically change our thinking, our playbooks, and our practices.

As H. G. Wells observed, "It is a law of nature we overlook, that intellectual versatility is the compensation for change, danger, and trouble. **An animal perfectly in harmony with its environment is a perfect mechanism.**"

To take this one stage deeper, we are not separate from our environment (though we experience the illusory feeling of separation or disjoint, as I've described above). We are part of the "perfect mechanism". Gregory Bateson (creator of the double-blind theory of schizophrenia) theorised that "man's only real self is the total cybernetic network of man **plus society plus environment.**"[6] We therefore have an interactive relationship with this environment. It influences us and we influence it. And it's important to note that when I say "environment" I don't mean just the planet and the ecosystem, as important as these are. I mean work environment, home environment, the area we live in (be it city, countryside, town, or mountain peak!). What social networks do we abide in? All of these are contributing factors to who we are and, of course, influence our adaption.

---

6   Quoted in *The Spectrum of Consciousness*, Wilber, Ken; 1977

As leaders, we create an environment for our people. We have a responsibility to role-model the adaptable behaviours necessary to thrive. To act accordingly and inspire courage and confidence to embrace uncertainty with curiosity and openness. In many ways, this is a sobering level of responsibility. In addition, this is not just a physical environment, such as an office space (and indeed, many businesses no longer have a literal physical environment, and work is conducted remotely), but an emotional, intellectual, and creative one. Our research shows that even if someone is innately adaptable and has trained their adaptability muscle, their environment can still significantly help or hinder their adaption.

As daunting as this makes the prospect of creating or curating a psychologically safe environment for our team-members, it is also empowering. By establishing the right environment, we can create a context in which our people can perform and grow into their very best.

AQ-ENVIRONMENT

AQ-Environment asks the question "When does someone adapt and to what degree?"

No doubt, as a leader, you have observed your team in their work-habitat. You have also probably had feedback from team-members about their environment (they may not use that word precisely, but you can identify the underlying meaning). This can range from the very pragmatic and physical, such as: "It would be nice if we had a coffee-machine in the office" to something more ambiguous or psychological, "I don't like the atmosphere here". As a leader, you have the responsibility of fielding these queries, assessing their relevance, and determining whether it is reasonable, possible, or positive to act on them and make a change in the environment.

From this we can deduce that environments are ever-shifting. As mentioned, we influence them and they influence us. Not only this, but we are the *curators* of our environment. Viewed another way: we create an environment that we then invite other people in to cohabitate. In the words of David Green, "Environmental Wellbeing is about living a lifestyle that is respectful and in harmony with our surroundings, nature, planet earth and all species living in it. **It is the bi-directional impact between us and our environment** whether built, natural, physical or virtual and includes our home, neighbourhood, workplace, community, country, planet and even the universe."

Green emphasises the holistic and multifaceted nature of an environment we've explored, rather than simply thinking of it as the ecology of the planet. When we begin to see environment this way, it opens up a whole realm of possibilities. We can, for example, begin to see how we might change our behaviours in certain contexts. Do we, for example, use different language when speaking with junior team members as opposed to senior ones? Should there be a difference? This is an obvious example, but it invites us to question how often we pay specific attention to these subtle differences. And what can we learn from the differences in our behaviours in different contexts?

And what about problematic environments? If we have a problematic environment at work (for example, a toxic culture of micro management and distrust), how do we approach that "bi-directional" relationship? Do we fight against the culture and try to give as little as possible, do we go with the flow and shrink to fit and comply, or do we provide alternatives? Whilst we obviously view flexibility as a good thing, too much flexibility can mean a loss of identity. If the bi-directional influence is imbalanced and you're the one being influenced all the time, but not able to influence others, then might this not have negative impacts on mental health and sense of Self?

Is there ambiguity in your organisation around when flexibility of process, language, and behaviours is seen as a benefit? For example, some may perceive a hyper-personalised, human-centred approach, whereas others may perceive the same actions through different eyes, instead seeing unfairness and inconsistency.

Of course, to a degree, our choice of environment may be limited by financial resources, location, education and many other factors. But even if we believe we cannot afford to move jobs or start our own business, we can make the most of the space and connections we have; this is saying nothing of the psychological environment we create: is it one of trust, of mutual respect, of openness to all views and ideas? In my view, our environment can be either the "**magical multiplier**" of success or its greatest subtractor.

This is not to say we should forever "stick it out" if we are truly unhappy. But we have the power to instigate change. Environments are powerful, and so are we, as elements in the system, we have the ability and responsibility to influence them for the better.

However, before we do that, the first step is to correctly identify the environment we operate in. No two businesses are alike. Nor are any two teams identical. We therefore have to establish what the current state of our environment is. How might the global movements I've described be impacting our industry?

Each problem and opportunity will have a different array of potential solutions. To unlock these solutions, it is a leader's responsibility to understand AQ and team adaptability at a deeper level.

WHAT IS ADAPTABILITY?

One of my preferred definitions is that

"ADAPTABILITY IS THE CAPACITY TO ADJUST ONE'S THOUGHTS AND BEHAVIOURS IN ORDER TO EFFECTIVELY RESPOND TO UNCERTAINTY, NEW INFORMATION, OR CHANGED CIRCUMSTANCES."

(Martin, Nejad, Colmar, & Liem, 2013).

We can immediately see the role of the environment in this definition. Our environment—especially in today's age—is constantly providing us with "new information" and "changed circumstances", to the point where we can feel whiplashed trying to keep up with it all. Not only are all these changes happening rapidly but we also tend to get notified about them in real time due to social media and instant messaging (though not always with a hundred percent accuracy, it must be said!). This naturally contributes to a feeling of overwhelm that is undoubtedly linked to the mental health crisis described in the first part of this book.

How often have you set your plan for the week, or for the day, diligently created your to-do list, only to be side-swiped by Slack messages, emails, and requests from your team members and clients/customers? It's a common problem we all experience, especially in our digitally interconnected world. We then face a choice of whether to rigidly and diligently stick to our plan, to our to-do-lists, or face a reality of day after day of constant "task shift" and workload "reactions": a slow death by a thousand paper cuts, stemming from lack of control, where we react to every squeaky wheel with a drop of oil, only to find when it comes to our previous (perhaps more important and energising tasks) that we have nothing left in the tank.

However, the good news is that we can adjust our thoughts and behaviours in order to be able to not only cope with what's changing but create success out of continual flux.

Countless studies, and the examples of history, have shown the key to longevity and success in any enterprise is adaptability. Indeed: "As a disposition and skill, adaptability is essential to an individual's psychological health, social success, and academic or workplace achievement." (National Institutes for Health, 2015).

BUT HOW DO WE KNOW HOW ADAPTABLE WE ARE? AND HOW CAN WE IMPROVE OUR ADAPTABILITY?

Many articles and leaders advocate becoming better at navigating change, but they miss out the how.

We have spent years collating the most robust scientific studies, the latest research, and observing cutting edge trends to formulate our comprehensive operating system for adaptability. From this, we understand AQ in terms of three interrelated master dimensions (the A.C.E model):

Ability *(your adaptability skills - How and to what degree one adapts)*

This is your adaption muscle group. It reflects how, over time, you can develop mastery in multiple or changing fields. This element encompasses your ability to be resilient and bounce back/or even forward from hardship, mental flexibility with holding opposing thoughts, your grit, as well as your mindset and ability to unlearn.

Character *(who adapts and why)*

This reflects a more innate (but contextual) aspect of adaptability quotient: your drivers, triggers, styles and willingness to adapt. Whilst you may be able to live with other characteristics in specific circumstances, we seek to understand preferences which channel flow and not compliance when it comes to why someone makes an adaptation or change. This important master dimension uncovers your profile, in motivation style, emotional range, extraversion, thinking style and the science of hope.

Environment *(how your environment can help or hinder your adaption - When one adapts, and to what degree)*

Your environment can either help or inhibit your adaption. This can typically be out of your control, yet you are part of the input! We explore areas such as company support, team support (psychological safety), work environment, emotional health, and work stress.

These three master dimensions further break down into seventeen sub-dimensions, which allows us to drill down into the distinct specifics, creating what we call our "**AQ Adaptiotic Table**™".

THE A.C.E MODEL OF ADAPTABILITY

THE 17 SCIENTIFICALLY VALID MEASURES OF ADAPTABILITY

THE AQ ADAPTIOTIC™ TABLE

AQ ABILITY

HOW AND TO WHAT
DEGREE DO I ADAPT?

1. GRIT
2. MENTAL FLEXIBILITY
3. MINDSET
4. RESILIENCE
5. UNLEARN

AQ CHARACTER

WHO ADAPTS
AND **WHY?**

6. EMOTIONAL RANGE
7. EXTRAVERSION
8. HOPE
9. MOTIVATION STYLE
10. THINKING STYLE

AQ ENVIRONMENT

WHEN DOES SOMEONE
ADAPT TO WHAT DEGREE?

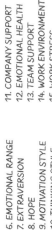

11. COMPANY SUPPORT
12. EMOTIONAL HEALTH
13. TEAM SUPPORT
14. WORK ENVIRONMENT
15. WORK STRESS

AI PREDICTIVE INDEXES

16. CHANGE READINESS INDEX
17. RESKILL INDEX

Ross Thornley THE **AQ** GUY

AQai.

THE SCIENCE OF ADAPTABILITY

We collaborated with Dr. Nicholas T. Deuschel, a research professor at Spain's leading Carlos III University and used one of the most robust models in organisational psychology (the input-process-outcome model) to create our tripartite Ability Character Environment model (or A.C.E.). In our case "adaptability" is the outcome, a result of a process and an input.

In our model, AQ-Character catalysts adaption (this is the "input"). In other words extraversion-introversion, our motivation style, our "personality traits", all create the impetus that drives us to adapt.

At the same time employees can learn new skills that allow them to adapt in different ways. This is AQ-Ability which also adds to the "input" stage of the model.

In addition, we are also influenced by our environment. We may have all the unique skills in the world to help us adapt, even a personality that is innately adaptable, but due to an inhibiting environment are unable to fully harness our AQ muscle. This is also another important "input".

We then experience the "process" in the form of adaptability behaviours, such as exploration (to seek out new and different ideas, and ways of doing things), exploitation (to utilise and maximise current resources and approaches), problem-solving, and creativity. And in a business context these manifest in a series of outputs: desired, predicted, and actual "outcomes". For example accelerated innovation, employee engagement, retention and reskilling with increased employee mobility and dynamic career pathways, learning and development culture, overall productivity and performance, together with health and wellbeing—stress and burnout reduction.

Understanding the specific flow, mix, and value of inputs, the resulting and chosen processes, and then the impact on outcomes will help us to continually leverage and optimise what we understand as our adaptability intelligence.

INPUT

AQ ABILITY
GRIT
MENTAL FLEXIBILITY
MINDSET
RESILIENCE
UNLEARN

AQ CHARACTER
EMOTIONAL RANGE
EXTRAVERSION
HOPE
MOTIVATION STYLE
THINKING STYLE

AQ ENVIRONMENT
COMPANY SUPPORT
EMOTIONAL HEALTH
TEAM SUPPORT
WORK ENVIRONMENT
WORK STRESS

PROCESS

ADAPTABILITY BEHAVIOURS

EXPLORE & TRANSFORM
EXPLOITATION - UTILIZE & IMPROVE
PROBLEM-SOLVING
CREATIVITY
COMMUNICATION LEVELS
LEADERSHIP STYLES
PRACTICES & PROCEDURES
SPEED OF LEARNING
DECISION MAKING
PRO-ACTIVE
REACTIVE

OUTPUT

ACCELERATED INNOVATION
PROFITABILITY
RELEVANCE
EMPLOYEE ENGAGEMENT
RETENTION
RESKILLING
EMPLOYEE MOBILITY
DYNAMIC CAREER PATHWAYS
LEARNING AND DEVELOPMENT
CULTURE
PRODUCTIVITY & PERFORMANCE
MENTAL HEALTH
WELLBEING, STRESS, BURNOUT
COLLAPSE / THRIVING

*EXAMPLES OF THE INPUT, PROCESS, OUTPUT MODEL
IN RELATION TO ADAPTABILITY*

Of course, this is only scratching the surface. But hopefully this basic overview has given you an idea of how the underlying principles of AQ are present and active in our lives.

What would you do differently looking at your team and business within the context of the three master dimensions?

THE AMYGDALA HIJACK

Now we know the rudimentary basics of AQ, and the three master dimensions that are constantly interacting and acting upon us (and in turn being acted upon *by* us), we can begin to harness this knowledge to better ride and navigate uncertainty and unpredictable changes.

How does adaptability really help us rise to the challenges posed by automation, AI, digitisation, the democratisation of information and knowledge, and industry transformation?

Naturally, when thinking about these things, it can evoke the "fear response".

I'm sure most of you will know what I mean by the fear response, but just to recap: this is when the amygdala, the primitive reptilian part of our brain, hijacks our thinking.

In their study, "Resilience Training That Can Change the Brain" (2018), Golnaz Tabibnia and Dan Radecki stated that: *"One of the challenges of consulting and coaching psychology is helping individuals, teams, and entire enterprises weather life and work stressors. These stressors can be one-time and acute, such as unexpected job transfer or job loss, or more chronic, such as bad bosses, broken peer relationships, and dysfunctional team members. Some people are more resilient than others in the face of such stressors, but many of the skills that make for resilience can be learned."*

In other words, without resilience, these "stressors", whether acute or chronic, can overwhelm us. And even worse: "cortisol and adrenaline are actually neuro-toxic; that is, too much of them and they can harm or even kill off brain neurons."[7] In other words, stress literally "shrinks" our brains!

When the amygdala has hijacked us, and we can only compute "fight or flight", our decision-making becomes significantly impaired. To make things worse, our brains are largely unable to differentiate between a life-threatening situation and one which is simply uncertain, unexpected, or unfamiliar. The brain offers the same response whether we are faced with talking in front of an audience of thousands or with a dangerous animal in the wild. This wouldn't be so much of a problem if we were easily able to dissipate this stress or fear re-

---

7 Psychologies Magazine; *Real Strength*; Capstone; 2017.

sponse, but in the modern world, we cannot act on the fight or flight impulse in most situations. Therefore, we find ourselves in states of stress for *extended periods of time*. This means our decision-making ability is impaired not just in one particularly stressful instance but often over the *longer term*. Hence, our careers, our mental and physical health, and our relationships are all impacted.

As organisational leaders, there are even deeper consequences for succumbing to amygdala hijack and failing to adapt than simply those of personal burnout or failure—distressing and profound as these moments can be. We can literally drive our companies into the ground, thereby impacting all our employees, partners, and clients.

To read more about this check out my big book:

DECODING AQ -
YOUR GREATEST
SUPERPOWER. A NEW
OPERATING SYSTEM
FOR CHANGE IN AN
EXPONENTIAL WORLD.

SHIFT FROM REACT TO RESPOND

One of the core tenets in mastering your AQ is shifting from reacting to responding during change.

It's hard, even if we're a naturally temperate and even-tempered person, not to give a knee-jerk reaction when one of our team comes running to us with a problem. As human beings, we're empathetic, we feed off the energy of those around us. Though we can't *literally* smell fear, we can detect it chemically—and fear can be infectious. They're worried about something, so we start to worry about it.

Or perhaps it's simply that, as a leader, you can see the changes coming down the pipeline, changes no one else has seen yet, and you're worried about how to break the news to everyone. This kind of anxiety can sometimes produce the opposite of a reaction: complete inaction, paralysis and uncertainty.

Instead of reacting to problems—or becoming paralysed—we want to respond. But what's the difference between a reaction and a response?

A reaction is often knee-jerk, like the old medical test where they strike the knee with a miniature hammer, to see you kick out, without intention. A reaction is not considered and often, sad though it is to say, makes matters worse. A response, however, is considered and appropriate, bringing the best of ourselves into a situation and circumstance. Remember we discussed in the opening how environments are contexts, and it's when our behaviour does not match the context that things go wrong. Reactions almost invariably clash with our environment. For example, at an important meeting, Person A says something mildly offensive. Person B is unable to contain their anger and explodes, angrily berating them. Everyone treats Person B like the bad-guy even though they were technically not the initiator of the conflict. This is because while what Person A said was offensive it could have been said in a calm manner appropriate to the context, whereas Person B's response was loud and abrasive and inappropriate to the meeting-context. If, however, Person B had instead been able to respond, rather than react, the meeting breakdown could have been averted.

By *responding*, we are able to match our environment and context, as well as act in a more considered way.

BUT HOW DO WE GET TO RESPONDING?

When we're driving a car and we want to change gears, before we can shift into the next gear, we have to disengage the motion source, and go via "neutral". Going into neutral is in some ways quite scary because the car is in a state of undefined direction in neutral. And if we stay in neutral too long, we'll most certainly never get anywhere! However, without neutral, we cannot get anywhere else—forwards or backwards—we cannot shift gears.

Another term I use for this is "limbo". When we receive external stimuli we deem to be threatening, or when we enter the unknown, our minds and bodies, like a car, realise that they need to shift gear, and we need to enter a moment of neutral or limbo. Ken Wilber described this phenomenon in a fascinating analogy:

"For instance, if I come up behind you and yell 'Boo!' there will be a few seconds wherein you remain still, even though you have heard me yell, and during this very brief time **you might feel a type of passive or quiet alertness**, but this feeling shortly explodes into a sensation of mild shock (or something similar) accompanied with an onrush of thoughts and emotions... **In those few seconds of passive awareness, your Energy was beginning to mobilize but it was not yet experienced as shock or mild terror**—it was pure and without form, and only later did it disintegrate into thoughts and emotions of shock and fright." [8]

---

8 Wilber, Ken; *The Spectrum of Consciousness*; Quest Books; 1977. p310.

It is by harnessing and leaning into this "passive" energy that we can quieten the fear response, and see the problem from a neutral standpoint.

So, when an employee comes to you with a unique or challenging problem, or indeed if you wake up to shocking news (such as the government deciding to regulate your industry) rather than succumbing to the amygdala hijack we can instead remodel from a reaction to a *response*.

Let me share a short tip, from my book **DECODING AQ**

"IN ORDER TO GIVE A **RESPONSE**, RATHER THAN SUCCUMBING TO A **REACTION**, WE MUST HARNESS "THE PULSE OF ADAPTIVE BEHAVIOUR". THIS "PULSE" MIGHT BE CONSIDERED A DEEP BREATH, A PAUSE. IT IS A MOMENT WHERE WE STEP BACK RATHER THAN ALLOWING THE MUSCLE-MEMORY OF OUR IN-BUILT RESPONSES TO TAKE OVER."

We must create comfort in the uncomfort, we must ride the unpredictable by leveraging a pause, the space in-between react and respond.

FIVE POWERFUL LANGUAGE RE-FRAMES TO SHIFT FROM REACT TO RESPOND

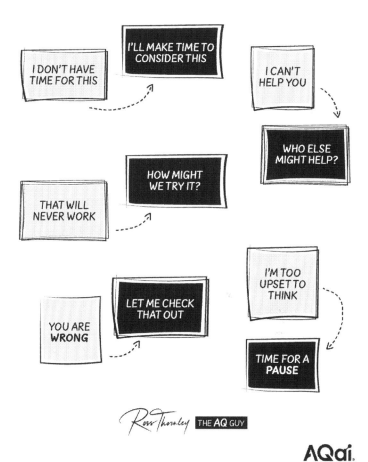

Ross Thornley · THE **AQ** GUY

AQai.

THE CORPORATE IMMUNE SYSTEM

As mentioned in the previous chapter, even if we—as an individual—are on-board with the concept of AQ and developing our adaptability muscles, we now face another challenge: how to make changes in such a way that the corporate immune-system response does not immediately reject and kill them! This may not be a difficulty all leaders face—those working in SMEs may have smaller teams with greater alignment and agility. However, even small businesses will encounter major issues if they are attempting radical levels of change and find themselves forcing change upon people who aren't ready to embrace it!

The corporate immune system is a fairly well-known phenomenon at this point, but it is worth unpacking in more detail, because it so directly ties in with our ability as transformational leaders to inspire and implement successful change.

Our immune system is designed to keep us safe from biological threats. However, sometimes, our body can be 'disrupted' by a virus or toxin, or we make a drastic change to our lifestyle or diet, and then the immune system has trouble identifying what is helpful and what is an enemy. This is an auto-immune disorder. It causes your defensive white blood cells to attack *everything* and dramatically weakens the body, sometimes even fatally. Hair falls out. Skin turns bloody and is covered in awful rashes. Energy levels plummet. The body is fighting a war with itself. This is a truly terrible thing to happen to anybody and it happens not just at a personal biological level, but also at a psychological and an organisational level.

But why? Why do people resist the very changes which might just save them?

Our AQ assessment measures individuals on a motivational continuum from playing-to-win to playing-to-protect. This might alternatively be considered as insight into whether someone is risk friendly or risk averse. People at the latter end of the continuum are more security-driven; they make calculated decisions based on risk assessment and protecting their assets. This isn't a "bad" thing, in any sense. Process and security-driven people can do well in roles that require meticulous precision or repetition or fastidious checking. We wouldn't want our accountant to take unnecessary risks with our finances, after all!

But as we prepare for technological displacement, many tasks we historically held dear will find themselves automated and replaced. Supporting the transition for those currently serving in these capacities will be a crucial challenge to overcome for virtually all businesses. Ensuring people feel connected, a sense of belonging and part of the collective, with a future contribution to serve, is a growing and important social aspect of every ethical business. We must commit to bringing all people with us into this new technology-driven world. However, someone who is more play-to-protect is unlikely to be a natural innovator, viewing change and innovation as a threat to security and well-being. Hence they can, almost literally, "attack".

Further to this, the ways in which an organisation introduces innovation can often magnify the immune system problem. Innovation and R&D teams are commonly equipped to deliver value through efficiency and productivity. This is where the innovations of yesterday have borne reward, and further embedding behaviours aligned to these practices.

When it comes to cutting-edge innovation, to creating radical breakthrough ideas, organisations often recruit external consultants after trying and failing internally. Together with acquisition strategies to accelerate technological adoption and market advantage. This dynamically different culture, when added to the core, can experience significant friction, stress, and disconnect. Risking the loss of great people, talent and experience with it.

To drive and achieve radical transformation ("radical" is in relation to your own current state) can be antagonising to the teams employed to maintain and grow "business-as-usual". To be honest, unless careful preparation and fertile ground exists within an organisation, most will fail at this type of far-horizon value creation. The freedom, trust, space, tolerance for failure rates, and facilitation required is often vastly underestimated. Asking your teams and people, who have been responsible for mitigating risk, to now take not a little but a lot of risk, to dream and give birth to crazy ideas, is no simple behaviour switch and requires brain gymnastics even for the most creative in your teams.

Either way, the organisation's immune system will often attack any and all initiatives that don't look like previous successes.

SO WHAT IS THE SOLUTION?

To help neutralise a corporate immune system attack, organisations previously fostered a culture of highly adaptable and experimental employees separate from the core, attempting to give them freedom, time, and space to experiment, removing the governance and reporting lines for approvals and allowing autonomous execution. This encouraged the transformation process, which, alongside outside collaboration, helped develop the company's future lifeline. Now the most successful organisations are investing in highly adaptable leaders and workforces across the organisation, not just at the edges and fringes, in a sand pit of their own. It must become a core competency for everyone within the organisation, to enable high levels of adaptability across the full spectrum, across the entire employee life-cycle, tenure, and hierarchy.

Simultaneously, bringing in measurement tools, platforms, and specialist coaches to psychologically and practically support your employees' transition with adaptability can be an effective way to reduce the negative immune system response. Transforming an organisation is not just about the organisation itself, but also about updating the mindsets and knowledge-base of the people who work for it so they are not "left behind" by organisational and industrial change. Together we must transform our organisation's antibodies (its white cells) into highly adaptable champions: red blood cells dedicated to driving innovation, and successfully navigating the wild waves of constant flux and change.

Changing the way people think, and the way you think, is not easy. It can be painful and sometimes torturous process that requires grit and determination. Figuring it out takes a level of bravery and, I would argue, a sense of adventure. Shifting our thinking shifts our reality. The same event or process that makes somebody very stressed, very awkward, very uncomfortable, can be joyful for someone else with the right mindset. It's a decision. It's not the path you take but the mindset with which you take the path. You could set out on a big adventure and it could be all about survival. Someone else could undertake the same adventure and it could be all about the experience and joy.

The adventure is still the adventure.

The *water* is not the difference, it's the *person swimming*.

And so I urge you in whatever adventure you undertake, whatever transformation you aim for, to know that the adventure is not the reason why it's stressful and hard or why you are encountering huge seemingly un-scalable obstacles. It is your perspective and mindset that create them. If you, as a leader, do it with optimism, do it with joy, do it with excitement and effervescence, that becomes infectious. It is important to make sure you're infecting your surroundings, your employees, your work-space, your colleagues, your friends—infecting them with energy, belief, vitality, and excitement.

Whilst I remain determined to create positive change in this world, I also recognise that there is no point achieving that change at the cost of all else. It's pointless to succeed in reaching a moonshot or a transformational goal, only to come out the other end near dead with exhaustion, stress, and a feeling of ill-will amongst the people you've been working with. To lose all of your emotional and physical resources and to kill the spirit of the team to get to the end is unhealthy and pretty unethical.

You want to arrive at each chapter of development with your energy and vitality still intact. Not only is this the best outcome for everyone, it's actually the best way to achieve the moonshot or transformation in the first place. When everyone is motivated, energised, and passionate, with purpose clearly aligned, you will harness the creative potential of those around. We can benefit from the 'red blood cell' effect of organisational champions.

SIX INSIGHTS FROM TOP LEADERS

As the host of the podcast Decoding AQ, it has been my privilege to interview over 100 of the world's top leaders on their stories and the power of adaptability. I wanted to distil the amazing insights many of these leaders offered in their interviews and pass on common trends I identified that were shared among them. Of course, every leader must ultimately forge their own path, but hopefully these examples will help inspire and inform your own practice and understanding.

1. LEAD FROM THE HEART.

Tony Martignetti, Founder of Planned Giving, author, and podcast host, talked about the importance of pursuing passion rather than merely going through the motions or making purely intellectual decisions. He describes how:

"In the beginning, I wasn't using my heart to drive my decisions, I was using my brain. But when you connect the two together, and

you start to make decisions from that place of 'What does my heart want?', 'What does my soul want from me?', then things start to shift."

Many business leaders can shy away from words such as "heart" and "soul" as they seem too ambiguous, airy fairy, or mystical, but of course human experience testifies to their reality, and we see a common theme in great leaders of the past and present that they absolutely engage with and move from the inner and spiritual self, not the external or image-driven self.

Eastern traditions such as Yoga and Buddhism have advocated for the power of connecting mind and body, heart and soul, for millennia, and even in the esoteric Western traditions we see the importance of listening to the "inner voice" emphasised time and again. In modern terms we often call this intuition, gut-instinct, or inspiration. Tony Martignetti beautifully describes inspiration as

"a communication with your soul's purpose."

When we look at it that way, the first person we have to be a leader to is ourselves!

2. CONTINUOUS LEARNING.

Perhaps the number one most-repeated maxim I heard from all the interviewees was the importance of continuous learning. In the words of James Sale, "Leaders are made in the crucible of learning, whether that learning is formally constructed or informally acquired."[9] Indeed, Cameron Herold, The Ceo Whisperer, said that,

"The leader controls the learning environment".

So leaders not only have to be lifelong learners themselves but they also curate the environment for others and set an example. **But how do we maintain an interest in continuous learning?**

Charlene Li, prolific author and digital transformation and disruptive leadership expert, said that

"When I don't have a good answer to something I get very curious."

It's fascinating that our language is encoded with so many warnings against curiosity, and yet curiosity is a defining trait

---

9   Sale, James; *Mapping Motivation for Leadership.*

of leadership success—exploring liminal spaces, new technology, and radical ideas. Voracious learning therefore perhaps stems from curiosity. **Diane Hamilton**, who authored the book *Cracking The Curiosity Code, said that, "There's the 'Curiosity-Gene' as coined by the Max Planck Institute. You know, it's something that you need as an individual, as a human, as an animal. I mean, if a bird only looked for berries in one bush it would run out of berries, and then die. So we need to have the curiosity to explore."*

This also connects with an openness to change. **Greg Verdino**, business futurist and digital transformation expert, describes himself as "**a student of change**", which I think is a powerful metaphor for the continuous learning process. **Tony Martignetti** describes how he read *"an unhealthy amount of self-help books"* when trying to transition into a new career—a wonderful oxymoron, but it illustrates how leaders are unafraid of absorbing new knowledge, and are eternally curious about what's out there. **Diane Hamilton** makes it clear how a *lack* of curiosity can result in complacency: *"I think what I was trying to do with the curiosity research was to get people to recognise that they weren't doing enough to explore to get out of 'status quo thinking'. That's kind of how I look at curiosity in the workplace, that we fall into this status quo way of doing things. And nobody's ever asking, why are we doing this? Why aren't we doing this? How can things be different?"*

Charlene Li shows how over time we can become stuck in our ways, refusing to leave what we have predetermined our "path" is. This of course prevents us from seeing other options. She advocates, *"having the humility to say, 'I don't know, is this the right path?"* She uses the analogy of driving: "Let me get off from driving the road and look at the map a little bit, look at the landscape and say, 'How has it changed? How has the world evolved?" This connects back with what we discussed in the chapter on AQ-Environment near the start of this book. Awareness of our surroundings is essential to navigating change; this is interrelated with our **Unlearning** ability, where we can let go of old narratives or identities to better serve present and future needs.

In the words of the 19th-century psychologist, William James, "To be fertile in hypotheses is the first prerequisite of discovery, and to be willing to throw them away the minute experience contradicts them is the next."

Tracy Brower, author of *The Secrets to Happiness at Work and Bring Work to Life,* reflects on how the Covid pandemic and significant societal shifts have influenced our relationship with identity, and our ability to change. *"Work is a primary way that we express our identity. But in order to move toward the future and stay agile, we don't want to become too entrenched in our current identity, we want to be able to move and shape and adapt and stretch that identity. I think those are some of the things that we're* *grappling with as individuals, and as groups and societies today."*

3. UNLOCKING POTENTIAL IN OTHERS.

All of the leaders I interviewed were focused on and interested in developing other people. Yes, they were keen to improve their own skills and capabilities and achieve success, but they wanted to show and inspire the way for others. So they in turn could unlock their inner potential and manifest the life they want. Aristotle used the word eudaimonia or "highest good" to describe this phenomenon, defining it as a human good desirable for its own sake, rather than for the furtherance of an agenda or ulterior motive.

Tony Martignetti outlines this beautifully: *"**Ultimately, what I really want is to make sure when people come to work, they feel inspired, they feel like they can have a fulfilling life**. And they can feel as though they're not wasting their time going to work by just collecting a paycheck, and **that they can ultimately unlock their full potential**."*

Tracy Brower also explores how problematic narratives around work can become barriers to unlocking potential: "We have this myth that work is drudgery… **in reality work is a place that we experience fulfilment. And the opportunity to express our talents, to express our capabilities, to contribute to our community.** We do that through work.

And we connect with people through work, even if we're introverts, right? We need those connections. And so work can be a context for so much fulfilment."

4. FORWARD THINKING.

Future orientation is an important prerequisite for any leader, even more so in our time of constant, global change.

Tom Cheesewright, futurist and author of Future Proof Your Business, says that, "a lot futurism is kind of thought of as being about, you know, jetpacks and brain implants and what's going to happen in 30-50 years time, and I do that stuff, it's really important. It's really interesting to lay out that vision of where you want to be: what are the opportunities? What happens if we don't intervene? **But actually, most of my work is at the two to five year range. What are those critical opportunities that we might not have seen? And what are those threats that are coming down the pipeline that, you know, might blindside us if we're not actively looking for them?"** Being able to anticipate "threats coming down the pipeline" is critical to steering an organisation through change. And whilst having a view of the long-term future is important, you also have to consider the more immediate future.

Forward thinking is also a prerequisite for happiness and wellbeing. The psychiatrist Gordon Livingston said, "Happiness requires something to do, someone to love, and something to look forward to." Without the prospect of a future, all our present-day endeavour feels quite meaningless. But this is not only about having a positive vision, but also being able to anticipate challenges that may come our way. This requires leaders to see the landscape as it truly is. The problem is that we tend to find our worldview obscured by bias. **Dr. Benjamin Hardy**, author of *Personality Isn't Permanent*, observed "We don't see the world as it is, we see the world as we are." In other words, we have a tendency to project our own flaws and meaning onto the external reality (Dr. Benjamin Hardy is an organisational psychologist, and one can see the psychological insight of this observation). Cutting through this illusion and seeing the truth is another core facet of leadership.

5. RADICAL TRUTH.

Enrique Rubio, founder of Hacking HR, talks about how sometimes the most valuable feedback is painful, *"The feedback that becomes the most important hurts at the beginning. But then you find the truth."*

Sometimes the truth can shatter our world. **Charlene Li** describes the challenges leaders face dealing with these seemingly world-ending revelations or challenges with a wonderful analogy: "When all the pieces are torn apart, are you hiding and ducking, trying not to get hit by those pieces, or are you jumping up as high as you can, grabbing those pieces, **and put-**

ting them back together again into the reality that you want to see? That is what leadership is. Leadership has nothing to do with the title. It has everything to do with your *mindset* that says, 'I see a change that needs to happen. And I will lead it.' And **leadership is fundamentally a relationship between those who aspire to create that change and the people who are inspired to follow them.** So you don't need a title to do that. You just need to be able to see the future."

6. OPTIMISM & HOPE.

Another common factor among all the leaders I interviewed was a sense of hope and optimism. **They believe positive change is possible.** The power of belief is so well documented, and in the West "faith" or "belief" is deemed one of the three pillars of Christianity as outlined by the Apostle Paul. Belief in a hopeful, positive outcome is directly linked with forward planning and visualisation. **Barry O'Reilly**, author of *Unlearn*, talks about how he became a best-selling author, given the fact he was dyslexic and struggled with English at school. He would ask himself: "In two or three year's time, if I was to smash it out of the park and become an amazing author, what would I be doing? Well, I'd be creating content all the time. I'd be making a blog every week, and if those blogs accumulate they turn into books. And by starting talking to myself in that way, I realised that the vision I was talking about was not sitting at a desk and typing, it was about creating content. And then I started to think: well, there're lots of ways to create content. You don't have to just sit there and type, especially when you start to pair it with technology." This led to **Barry O'Reilly** writing his books via dictation. By visualising the future in which he was already a successful author, he was led to the answer of how to achieve it.

John D. Anderson observed: "80% of what I write down comes true by merely writing it down and then stating it out loud. And now there's data and evidence that supports all that." The conviction to write down a goal is *itself* a large step towards that goal manifesting, but only when writing down the goal is backed by genuine belief, commitment and courage of course.

Tracy Brower highlights the simple power of belief beautifully with an amusing anecdote: "I'll never forget, I got a recruiter who called me towards the latter part of my twenty years at Herman Miller. And she said to me, 'Tracy, after twenty years, do you think you'd be capable of making a change?' And I thought, 'Oh, my gosh, of course, the answer is yes.'" Tracy believed in her own power to change even after a long time in the same role. She was able to decouple from a limiting sense of identity and envision a future of change and further growth.

But this optimism also applies to our external or organisational goals. Earl Nightingale said, **"EVERY WORTHY GOAL EVER SET IN THE HISTORY OF MANKIND HAS BEEN ACHIEVED."** An encouraging thought!

THEORY INTO ACTION

We can see how the abilities, characteristics, and mindsets outlined by top leaders seamlessly correlate with the sub-dimensions of AQ, particularly Mental Flexibility, Unlearning, Mindset, and Hope.

This is further supported by the findings of a 2015 survey, "Potential: Who's Doing What", which identified "learning agility" as "the most frequently used criterion to measure leadership potential". "Learning agility" consists of "experimentation, self-reflection, leveraging individual strengths, continuous improvement, mindfulness, and mentally connecting experiences obtained in one situation to different challenges in another."[10] Needless to say, all of these map to AQ-muscles and the skills we have identified.

---

10 De Meuse, Kenneth P.; "LEARNING AGILITY: ITS EVOLUTION AS A PSYCHOLOGICAL CONSTRUCT AND ITS EMPIRICAL RELATIONSHIP TO LEADER SUCCESS"; *Wisconsin Management Group, Minneapolis, Minnesota*; Consulting Psychology Journal: Practice and Research, 2017, Vol. 69, No. 4, 267–295.

But if this is the theory, then how do we practically implement these into an organisational environment? How do we inspire teams that have existed—perhaps for a long time—within a given framework without triggering the corporate immune-system response, and without destroying the organisational equilibrium?

One answer to this is "visibility". "What gets measured gets managed" as Peter Drucker once said. We can't change positively if we don't know what's wrong. If you were allergic to a certain type of food, but didn't know which item it was making you sick, then your only recourse would be to cut things out of your diet one by one until the allergic reactions stopped (taking a huge risk with your health in the meantime!). Whilst you might eventually get to the solution, the road is extremely painful, and you may not even have survived long enough to see the end, depending on the severity of your allergy. This is an apt metaphor for how many businesses go about trying to enact change. They keep making cuts and changes, hoping each time the underlying mindsets, behaviours, and issues will be fixed. What we need are diagnostic tools that help us uncover the invisible, show us what the allergy is, so we can avoid it and build better nutrition all around.

This circles right back to the opening of this book, where we talked about how an awareness of our environment is the first step to making positive change. We can now take this one step further: What if you were able to measure your environment accurately? What if you had a metric that could put a numerical value on it? And a numerical value of the adaptability of your people?

At AQai, we've developed the first ever holistic measure of AQ and diagnostic tools (AQme and AQTeam) to help organisational leaders steer their businesses through the most significant period of change in human history.

BY INTRODUCING AQ INTO YOUR WORKPLACE, YOU CAN:

→ CONNECT TO YOUR EMPLOYEES ON A DEEPER LEVEL THAN TRANSACTIONAL—AKA, ON AN EMOTIONAL LEVEL, LEADING FROM THE HEART AND CONNECTING WITH WHAT YOUR PEOPLE CARE ABOUT.

→ GAIN ACCESS TO DATA THAT ALLOWS YOU TO CONTINUOUSLY MAP YOUR EMPLOYEES THROUGH THEIR ADAPTABILITY OR CHANGE JOURNEY— EMBRACING CONTINUOUS LEARNING.

→ UNLOCK YOUR EMPLOYEES' FULL POTENTIAL BY GIVING THEM ACTIONABLE SELF-INSIGHT.

→ AND CULTIVATE AN ENVIRONMENT OF CONTINUOUS IMPROVEMENT, OPTIMISM, AND FUTURE-PROOFING BY ENSURING EVERYONE IS CHANGE-READY, AND NO ONE IS LEFT BEHIND.

TO FURTHER EXPAND ON THIS, HERE ARE SOME WAYS AQ CAN SYNERGISE WITH AND MULTIPLY MANY OF YOUR EXISTING PROCESSES.

1. Do you currently map your employees' development and career journeys? If so, how might a regular AQ assessment augment this process if it was integrated with the mapping and planning? Giving powerful insight into blind-spots of potential.

2. Are your diversity, inclusion and engagement initiatives achieving the outcomes and organisational wide shifts you are seeking? How might the support to improve mental flexibility, and transform past biases with unlearning programs, lead to enhanced environmental safety and allow for greater impact?

3. What tools do you currently use with your employees? DISC, Predictive Index, EQ, Strengthsfinder? Which of them synergise with AQ? And, to put this in a more empowering way: what points of overlap interest you? Are you fascinated by the role of motivation or EQ in adaption, or how the Big 5 correlate with AQ-Character? You may not have all the answers at this point, but consider what evokes your curiosity, as it may lead you to surprising revelations and delightful opportunities.

4. How are you building the next wave of high potential talent, to drive greater retention and support radical employee mobility? Do you have a current skills matrix which would benefit from predictive insights on individual and team change readiness, with a converging re-skill index data point? How might AI-powered AQ insights create enhanced visibility for your management teams?

5. How do you currently measure employee engagement, satisfaction, or the state of thriving and happiness? Do you use questionnaires, or do you take their testimony as an accurate measure? How might introducing insights into the emotional health, work stress, and psychological safety of your teams enhance your outcomes? Would it give you more visibility and actionable points? Would it give you positive data points with which to measure and improve the success-rate of your leadership initiatives?

6. Consider what your most commonly asked questions are. What do employees ask you over and over again? Do the questions have a relationship with AQ and the "three master dimensions" of: Ability, Character, and Environment? How might this knowledge empower you to provide answers to these questions? How might using this tripartite model give your employees a framework for understanding their challenges? And thrive in uncertainty.

7. Are you running leadership workshops and training programs? How might you integrate a program of development around adaptive behaviours? To unlock an ambidextrous organisation? That can simultaneously exploit the core and explore the radical innovations of tomorrow to ensure sustainability and growth.

These are just a few ways in which you can begin to explore the intersections between your existing practice and AQ. Whilst we cannot provide all the answers, deepening your understanding of AQ can only lead to new frontiers and possibilities.

DIGITAL TRANSFORMATION

To provide a concrete example of how AQ can level-up your organisational efficacy, I'll share a case study of a program we ran for UNIDO, the United Nations Industrial Development Organisation.

Jason Slater, Chief of IT & Digitisation UNIDO, said that:

"WE KNEW THAT WE NEEDED TO PREPARE OURSELVES FOR THE FUTURE, BUT WE DIDN'T KNOW HOW TO PREPARE."

UNIDO had invested heavily in traditional financial management, and needed to re-focus their finance department on digital transformation to enhance their digital readiness, technology adoption, efficiencies, and innovation.

OUR KEY GOALS WERE:

→ TO ACCELERATE DIGITAL TRANSFORMATION

→ INCREASE EFFICIENCY AND EFFECTIVENESS OF PROCESSES

→ TO IDENTIFY KEY OPPORTUNITIES FOR LEADERSHIP LEARNING AND DEVELOPMENT

THE APPROACH:

As part of the VBO Finance Conference for Vienna-based UN organisations (inc. IAEA, UNIDO, UNDOC, CTBTO, which employ over 5000 people from over 125 countries) the team at AQai led the 'innovation & adaptability' track, with multiple keynotes, workshops, and presentations delivered over 2 days, sharing key data on the future of work, exponential technologies, and the latest research on the number one most in demand skill of adaptability.

Jason Slater, at the time, Chief of Financial Management, sanctioned his department to be taken through AQ assessments, workshops, and team coaching, to help employees shift to a culture of unlearning, experimentation, and wider horizon thinking.

RESULTS & IMPACT:

Within 6 months of the AQ pilot program, the team created an environment of increased experimentation and innovation, creating automated finance bots to take over repeatable tasks that were using up valuable human thinking time. With extra people hours saved, the team formed an Innovation hub with other departments and agencies, with a mission to raise $20m for funding UN SDG initiatives. With a radical ambition to leverage blockchain for all future financial transactions.

→ NEW BOTS, RPA AND BLOCKCHAIN TECHNOLOGIES WERE DEPLOYED TO DRIVE EFFICIENCIES, WITH LESS FRICTION AND PUSHBACK.

→ THE PARTNERSHIP WITH AQAI STARTED IN 2019 AND ENABLED RAPID RESPONSE TO COVID-19, WHERE PROCESSES WERE REIMAGINED WITHIN DAYS TO ENABLE WORK FROM HOME.

→ ADOPTION OF NEW WAYS OF WORKING WERE LED BY THOSE FROM THE AQ PILOT PROGRAM, ENSURING CONTINUED DELIVERY OF SERVICES TO MEMBER STATES.

THE IMPACT FOR UNIDO

→ <u>CONCEPT TO CO-CREATE AN SDG INNOVATION CENTRE WITH VIENNA UNIVERSITY</u>

→ 20% RESOURCE TIME SAVED IN THE FINANCE DEPT.

COMMENTS:

"It was to my surprise that such a thing like AQai existed and has now enabled us to measure ourselves, to benchmark our data against what is considered to be best practice in the area of change and adaptability. So that was one of the key drivers for us in the UN system at large."

"What came out very, very clear from the assessment program was that we needed a different type of environment to enable our team to learn, but importantly, also to unlearn certain things that have been institutionalised."

Jason Slater, Chief of IT & Digitisation UNIDO

CONCLUSION

The journey of a thousand miles begins with a single step. Leadership is a complex and important topic, one that will continue to be relevant so long as human beings exist. Likewise, AQ is no ordinary subject of study, we are committed to unlocking the skills, mindsets, and environments to ensure everyone can thrive, a world where everyone can have complete future confidence no matter the context, and that no one is left behind. This book is an all-too-brief glimpse into the science and principles of AQ and how they correlate with transformational leadership. In reality, each sub-dimension of AQ is a life's work to understand and improve. Angela Duckworth's book entitled *Grit* is a testament to that fact! This means it can be daunting to know where to start.

The temptation, having done an AQme assessment, is to dive immediately into our weakest sub-dimension (for example, perhaps we have low Resilience) and then frantically begin trying to improve it. However, this is a reaction, not a response!

I personally recommend starting with understanding the situation and overall goal, or desired outcomes. These are the lenses through which we can then bring meaning using the three master dimensions: AQ-Ability, AQ-Character, and AQ-Environment. If we understand how these "three inputs" interrelate, and serve the specific situational objectives, then we can leverage the best results for ourselves, our teams and for our organisations.

It is my firm belief that in harnessing AQ, we can unlock our greatest potential, as individuals and as a species.

If, as a leader, you answer the following 7 questions with a hell yes, then running an AQ pilot program will be the greatest multiplier of transformational success you can gift your teams.

---

1.   You proactively want to expand the support for the mental health and wellbeing of your workforce, recognising they need help to successfully navigate the massive changes ahead.

2.   You see innovation not just as needed but as a critical competitive advantage that will become ever more valuable through each market change.

3.   You recognise we are living in a VUCA* world, and invest in the learning and development of your people to provide relevant and happy futures, for both your people and your organisation. *(volatility, uncertainty, complexity, and ambiguity)

---

4. You have over 25 employees.

5. You are committed to invest in understanding and improving the adaptability of your leaders and workforce. Improving your people's resilience, mindset, and motivation. Cultivating hope, engagement, and reducing stress.

6. You are committed to co-elevation and collaboration, looking for new ways to leverage relationships for the health and growth of society at large.

7. You see an urgent need to take action now, reimagining and engaging your organisation in creating collaborative solutions to expand your future value and vision.

THE AQ PILOT PROGRAM

Simply put this is an **8 week bespoke adaptability pilot program.** To help leaders like you, to retain and develop your employees, improve wellbeing, and begin to strengthen your whole organisation's positive relationship with change.

The AQ Practitioner & Pilot Program promotes effective and engaging adaptability data, to help you identify hidden strengths and opportunities to enhance employee's abilities and skills to navigate change, at an individual, team, and organisational-wide level.

HOW DO WE DELIVER VALUE?

Having the largest and fastest growing network of adaptability-certified consultants in the world, combined with our unique people-data science, this short program is guaranteed to deliver results.

We train, certify, and empower Talent Professionals and Leaders like you. Our hybrid learning experience involves 45 lessons, workbooks, and 4 hours of live training. Resulting in your AQ Certification with a bunch of SHRM credits too.

As we all know learning and practice is one thing, embedding and activating is another. So if you choose our AQ Pilot we shift to the practical application in your organisation, so your newly minted knowledge doesn't gather dust in a corner of your mind, or on a shelf, but it's actually implemented with you.

So, learn by DOING, apply your new AQ skills and activate a pilot programming YOUR organisation, led by one of our Certified Adaptability Professionals and join companies such as Microsoft, Amazon, and LVMH in being some of the very first to leverage AQ solutions.

WHY NOW?

Change is happening faster than many businesses' ability to adapt.

And did you know adaptability intelligence, your AQ, is the number one most desired skill according to Linkedin Learnings annual report, and Forbes, and we believe the best predictor of life satisfaction and career success?

Employees, leaders, and companies in every corner of the world are struggling to keep pace with the changes required to stay relevant, let alone thrive. We are seeing the highest levels of workplace stress, and accelerating talent attrition.

Challenges like the great resignation, hiring freezes, massive proposition pivots, and entirely re-writing the remote and hybrid working playbook, not to mention being expected to transition to newer and newer systems and technologies constantly.

Leaders are still right in the middle of these overwhelming changes, where employees are demanding better working cultures and more flexibility; Wellbeing, performance and results are under immense pressure.

Don't let your high potential talent and most valuable leaders down. You can make a difference, right now. Not in years, or months, but within weeks.

WHAT NEXT?

Visit our website and speak to our team at AQai to learn more and even **get a made for you business case template** to help gain buy-in. *https://aqai.io/organizations/aq-pilot*

Pilot Program for Organisations

Includes certification

**2 week
AQ Practitioner
Certification**

+

**6 week
Pilot Program
Launched**

Includes :

✓ AQ Practitioner Certification course

✓ AQ assessments for your team

✓ People data and analytics, from science backed-research

✓ Team report and debrief

✓ Pilot program launched within your organisation to prove impact

45 on-demand lessons   **4** hours of live training   **11** SHRM credits available   **4** yrs of research, science & application

Phase 1

Get Certified – Train & perfect your skills in AQ

Train and certify internal HR Professionals in AQ (Adaptability Intelligence) before launching a pilot program within your organisation working alongside an AQ Professional Partner. We work together to tailor the right approach and program for your needs.

A quick look in side AQ Pratitioner Certification..

100% Online	Duration	
10% One-to-One	Varies depending on your time constraints and the pace in which you wish to complete the course.	Module 1 : **Introduction**
65% Self Paced		Module 2 : **Application & Model**
25% Live Session	**typically 2-3 weeks**	Module 3 : **AQ Environment**

 Phase 2

Activate Pilot – We help you launch a tailored AQ Pilot program

We help you launch a pilot AQ Adaptability training program in your organization, working with a selected Certified Partner from our worldwide community. By unlocking the power of AQ you can demonstrate impact and uplift in team & business performance.

1	2	3	4	5
Onboard & Setup	Select & Match	Launch & Collect	Data Intelligence & Analysis	Debrief & Activate
WEEK 1	WEEK 2 & 3		WEEK 4	WEEK 5

"

*For us it was obvious: if we as a company want to effectively surf the wave of
constant change, we will have to strengthen our employees' adaptability and
change leadership.*

*For us the AQme assessment is an essential part of our Accelerating Leaders' self-
awareness journey that allows them to improve their adaptability and take concrete
actions on their abilities.*

- Nick Price, Founder

"

Join some of the most ambitious companies on the planet

ABOUT THE AUTHOR

R oss Thornley is an exponential leader, futurist, and adaptability pioneer. Living in the UK with his wife Karen, their two dogs, bee hive and rescue chickens, he balances the rapid technological world with a peaceful life in the New Forest, where they grow dozens of fruit and vegetables for their simple vegan lifestyle.

"Coach, Mentor, Entrepreneur and 'AQ' Pioneer. Author of Moonshot Innovation & AQ Decoded. Ross's work is opening up new frontiers in workplace education. Leveraging conversational AI and predictive analytics his company's platform enables people, teams and organizations to successfully navigate accelerating change. His ability to contextualize diverse and complex subjects, inspire and engage audiences makes him a highly sought after international speaker." **WALL STREET JOURNAL.**

At AQai, he is co-founder, CEO and master trainer, in flow when building the army of highly engaged and committed pioneers. Training over 170 coaches in the science and power of human adaptability in the first year of the program.

A passionate and prolific creator and educator. Amassing over 10,000 hours of workshop design, facilitation and keynotes over two decades. A serial-entrepreneur launching and growing multiple businesses across; innovation, branding, training and technology.

AQai (2018) transforming the way people and organisations adapt to change. Launching the first AQ (Adaptability Quotient) assessment and personalised digital coaching platform leveraging AI.

An eternal optimist, champion of abundance, and international speaker, he is the founder of 6 companies, including *RT Brand Communications* (2000, exit 2017), a globally trusted strategic branding agency that has worked with UN Volunteers, Thomson Reuters, Sony and numerous other blue chip clients; *Mug For Life®* (2009) a UK designed and manufactured reusable coffee cup, helping companies like HSBC, Amex, NHS, Science Museum and dozens of universities to achieve more sustainable waste policies by reduce single use disposable coffee cups and planting trees through their UK program; *Leaps®* *Innovation* (2017), a rapid, proven approach to moonshot innovation, idea generation and business challenges that empowers organisations to validate effective strategies, campaigns, new proposition development and solutions within days.

He's been a Strategic Coach® FreeZone Frontiers™ and 10X Member, Abundance A360 Member, and Singularity University Executive Program Graduate. Always excited by ambition, collaboration, and new models of thinking. Looking to connect ambitious people and solutions with communities, through creativity, intelligence and innovation.

His MTP is

TO UNITE, INSPIRE AND ACCELERATE THE BEST OF ALL HUMANITY.

www.AQai.io
https://www.linkedin.com/in/rossthornley/

OTHER BOOKS BY THE AUTHOR

MOONSHOT INNOVATION

Learn how to thrive in a world of exponential change and fulfil your highest good with a moonshot ambition.

DECODING AQ

Unlock the secrets of adaptability intelligence to harness your greatest superpower.

THE COACH'S ULTIMATE GUIDE TO LEVERAGING ADAPTABILITY

Drive client value with seven powerful principles to navigate change and leverage adaptability.

Notes:

Notes:

Notes:

Notes:

Notes:

Printed in Great Britain
by Amazon